To Margaret

from Alien *to* Italo-Scot

by

LEONELLA LONGMORE

Leonella Longmore

For my grandchildren
Anthon Melissa Chiara Luca

That they may never forget their roots

First Published 2016
Copyright © Leonella Longmore 2016

ISBN Number: 978-1-5262-0410-3

British Library Cataloguing in Publication Data
available from the British Library

Published by Leonella Longmore
Typesetting and layout by David Trujillo-Farley

Front Cover: The old Ness Café & Temporary Bridge

Page iv: Borgo Val di Taro (view)

Page vi: Map—The Homeland

Back Cover: The Locarno

CONTENTS

APPENDIX

Italian Businesses (Inverness) 1938–1939

Italian Detainees—Inverness Prison 1940

Acknowledgements

Image Acknowledgements

1. Borgo Val Di Taro

FOREWORD

This story is not a precise history of Italian immigrants who came to settle in Scotland during the last century. It is the tale of one of the many families who, driven by poverty, had to seek a new way of life far from the people they knew and loved. My parents were amongst those who arrived in the north of Scotland in the 1920s. Their feelings of bewilderment and nostalgia were conveyed to me as I grew up: the look of melancholy in their eyes, the ever-present ache in their hearts. But as a child, I did not understand. Belatedly, I am attempting to tell part of their story: of the resilience and courage with which all immigrants, past and present, face and overcome the difficulties of life in a foreign country.

Although I have a wealth of personal family documents, correspondence and photographs, I have enjoyed the encouragement and support of members of the Inverness Italian community who have openly spoken of their personal experiences, some of which I quote. I share with them sorrows and joys of by-gone days.

We are fortunate to have information available through the Highland Archive Service, the Inverness Public Library Reference Room and in the records and photographs held by Am Baile and the Highland Photograph Library. My thanks go to the staff who kindly helped me in my research; to William Morrison who guided me through the many images in 'Inverness Remembered'; to my husband Bryan and sons Bruno and Marco, whose constant help and encouragement are invaluable. For illustrations I have used my own photographs and documents and have given acknowledgements where other sources are known to me. I apologise for any omissions.

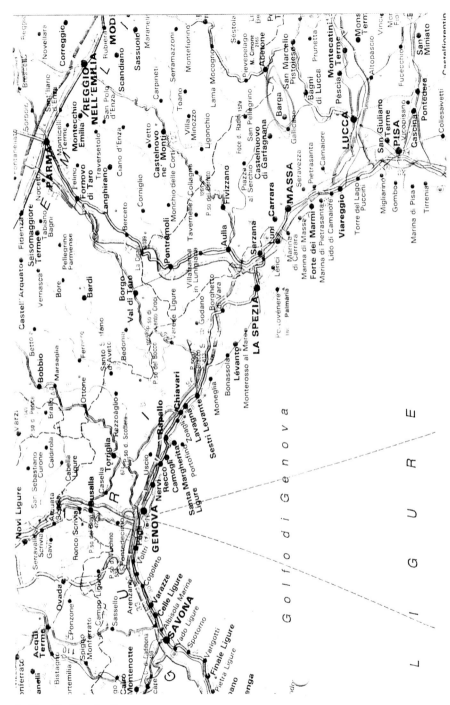

2. Map (The Homeland)

CHAPTER ONE

Alien

'No, you can't play with us! You're a Tally!' Who were these playmates who now looked at me accusingly? One, in particular, stared with undisguised hostility. Her dislike of my being Italian was about to put an end to the innocent belief that I belonged in the group surrounding me. At the age of five I felt the hurt but did not understand the rejection. It took time to heal and to understand. And with the healing and understanding came a wish to tell the story of an Italian immigrant family who arrived in the North of Scotland many years ago. Like all immigrants throughout the ages, my father and mother came with the dreams and ambitions of those who long to escape from a life of little opportunity.

So this Tally will tell a story which is part of Invernessiana although the names are not those that appear in the many antiquarian books on old Inverness. A story of a people who, like the Highlanders, had to leave their homesteads to seek a new life abroad, a people who, like the Highlanders came from beautiful mountainous regions, a people who, like the Highlanders thought with longing of the land they had left behind. The abrupt change of a life-style is traumatic for those facing an incomprehensible language and unfamiliar customs. And, once settled in a new and strange land what do they do to retain a sense of identity? They develop an overwhelming love for the land in which they were born and cling to those closest to them, those who understand and share their love.

I know—for I am the daughter of Italian economic migrants.

Dante, the greatest exile of all time, knew how to express the feelings of all who are forced to leave their homeland;

> *Tu proverai sì come sa di sale*
> *Lo pane altrui, e com'è duro calle*
> *Lo scendere e'l salir per l'altrui scale.*

(You shall find out how salt is the taste of another man's bread, and how hard is the way up and down another man's stairs). *Paradiso xvii*

3. *Roma, Disegno di Benito Jacovitti*

CHAPTER TWO

The Italians Are Coming

Millions of emigrants who suffer the dread of having to leave the land of their birth believe that theirs is a unique experience: millions of emigrants, past and present, are troubled by a vague ache deep within. The experience is not unique, the ache will never quite disappear. But another awareness grows as they strive to make a new life for themselves: a feeling of having found the courage to overcome a fear of the unknown. We see this today with the movement of peoples being a constant theme in the history of Europe.

Over the centuries Italians arrived in the UK for reasons of trade, commerce or diplomacy. In the 19th and 20th centuries they came to escape from poverty.

The history of their arrival goes back to 1290 when Edward I expelled the Jews from his kingdom. This vacuum was filled by Italian bankers—the Lombardi—who set up shop in London and whose expertise and reputation led to the naming of Lombard Street in the City. It was here that our old coinage system was established:

lire, soldi, denari = £ s d

Then, as Murdoch Rodgers wrote in 1981:

'Italians have a long and varied history in Scotland. They first came to prominence in the wake of the Renaissance in the 16th century and it has been established that James IV and James VI, both much influenced by Italian culture, employed Italian minstrels to entertain the literati who attended the court at Holyroodhouse. Royal favour of a different kind was bestowed upon the ill-fated David Rizzio, ex-Piedmontese musician and counsel to Mary, Queen of Scots. But it was in the 18th century that Italian culture achieved its strongest hold.'

A contemporary writer claimed that:

> 'every girl in Edinburgh who plays the piano learns Italian and Italian masters are to be found in every street'. The greatest of those was the renowned Italian tenor, Guisto Ferdinando Tenducci, who settled in Edinburgh in 1770.'

Rodgers also tells us that the poet Fergusson regarded the popularity of Italian culture as a threat and satirised the dandies who followed Italian fashion as 'macaronies'.

This last epithet surprised me: one of the terms of derision to which I had been subjected during World War Two. I had not realised this one dated back to the 18th century!

The 19th century saw famous, political figures seeking refuge in Britain:

- Giuseppe Mazzini, champion of the movement for Italian Unification, il Risorgimento;
- Gabriele Rossetti, poet and father of the famous painter and poet, Dante Gabriele Rossetti and his equally famous sister poet, Christina Rossetti;
- Antonio Panizzi, Principal Librarian of the British Museum and designer of its famous Reading room. He was the first Italian to be knighted.

These are some examples of the Great and Mighty.

But it is the Humble and Insignificant who were to bring about changes to the way of life in the towns and cities of Scotland. They came from the land and the small hill towns of Emilia and Tuscany. They are the unsung—and they are my people.

CHAPTER THREE

Origins of the Italian Community in Britain

Traced from 1830, the influx into London was of the impoverished and unskilled peasants and smallholder farmers. Many who came to Scotland were from the Appenine Mountain regions of Emilia and Toscana—an area around Barga in the Garfagnana, extending the length of the Serchio Valley into the hilltop hamlets of Modena and Parma and the coastal villages around la Spezia.

4. Barga Cathedral

Another group that eventually came up to Scotland were from the area around Cassino, the present-day provinces of Frosinone and Isernia. Finally, a later and smaller group arrived from Friuli near Venice in the province of Pordenone. With isolated exceptions very few of this group came to the North.

Since my parents came from the Appenines, I shall write of the region I know best: Emilia-Toscana.

Here you find a land of gentle hills topped with tiny hamlets that overlook fertile valleys and abound with castles and churches that go back to the early Middle Ages; here you will discover anonymous paintings by unkown Renaissance artists

5. Bardi

whose work adds to the perfection of the unadorned Romanesque architecture. From here you will see the stately poplar tree of the plain changing to the omnipresent cypress tree that forms the tapestry that is Toscana.

Mark Twain wrote:

> 'Lump the whole thing! say that the Creator made Italy from designs by Michelangelo.'

I would add that in Tuscany the Creator also had in mind the landscape paintings of Leonardo da Vinci.

So from these small mountain towns where life was a constant struggle came the immigrants, first arriving in London in the 1820's and early 1830's. As the era of train travel had yet to come, almost all of them walked to 'the promised land'. They followed a route North through Italy to the Alps, crossing at Chambery into France and then on to Paris before crossing the Channel for London. The migrants used to say they accomplished this marathon using 'il cavallo di San Francesco' (Shank's pony).

6. Borgo Val Di Taro—Gate 19th Century   *7. Shank's Pony*

CHAPTER FOUR

Chain Migration

It is not surprising to learn that the immigrants had intended to come as seasonal workers, for few wanted to leave forever the beloved fatherland. But because of the distance and expense involved, they did not take long to realise they would have to settle down in an unfamiliar environment, that their new way of life was here to stay. No matter how hard and dispiriting had been the work they once knew, starry-eyed visions of a fading dream remained with them. One craving kept them going: the desire to bring over their immediate family and close relatives. That way they would bring understanding and love once more into their lives, they would have someone to share the hardships and setbacks, they would not be alone to face an indifferent people and a difficult language.

Thus began what is called Chain Migration—a trend whereby those established in a foreign country send over for family members to join them.

As we are witnessing today, the economic migrants are open to exploitation by unscrupulous gang masters: the 'padroni' of yesteryear.

The *padrone* was essentially a labour boss. Often he would go back to Italy for recruitment purposes—usually to his own village or area from which he had come and in which he was known. He

8. *Organ Grinder*

would contract with parents for their children to come and work for him with food and lodgings and the promise of a lump sum to be paid at the end of a period, usually two or three years.

This system lent itself to mistreatment of the young, with very young boys being sent to assist the street entertainers; the Barrel Organ Grinders with their monkeys trained to dance and beg. Many of the organ-grinders came over for the summer only and needed boys to collect the money and push the organ as they wound their way round the streets. We have idealised visions of organs playing lively Neapolitan songs and operatic arias. The picture is not quite so idyllic for organ grinders were not always welcome. There was a belief that many of them deliberately played out of tune so the exasperated pedestrians and shop-keepers would pay them to 'move off their patch'. For the young boys the working day was long and tiring—9.00am–11.00pm— with their earnings going to the padroni who were then able to afford to retire to Italy. In the 19th century this exploitation was well known and widely opposed. Giuseppe Mazzini was amongst those who worked against the ruthless trade in Italian children.

But old habits die hard. Renzo Serafini, a well-known Barghigiano/Invernessian, used to talk of the callous treatment endured by young men even into the early 20th century:

'The padroni used to take over workers from Barga, maybe they had eleven, twelve, fourteen workers. In one room there were three double beds and the first to arrive back from work lay down three to a bed. The poor souls who arrived last had to sleep on the floor.'

9. Knife Grinder

In the mid 19th century the wave of immigration included groups of semi-skilled craftsmen:

The ARROTINI—knife-grinders from Val Rendena (now in Trentino in the Italian Dolomites—then part of the Austro-Hungarian Empire)

They went to the cities—especially London—and were very much in demand with the large households, hotels, restaurants. The grinders were originally carried on the mens' shoulders; later they were dragged on a cart through dirty streets. By 1929 they had modernised: their sharpening wheels were carried round the towns and cities on bicycles.

The MOSAIC & TERRAZZO workers. They mostly came from the Friuli region of northern Italy near Venice and again were in great demand for work in large private and public buildings. The first terrazzieri to gain an international reputation were those who constructed the floors in the Peace Palace in the Hague (1913). Being highly specialised workers, they represented the upper class of the labour force.

In 1924 Robert F Foerster wrote:

> 'It is common to find them at work on the most exacting tasks, ensuring the neatness of appearance, of the most ambitious public and private structures.'

The FIGURINAI. They were the makers of small statues and figurines in plaster of Paris. Originating almost exclusively from the province of Lucca in Toscana, they came mostly from two communes, one of which is Barga.

10. Figurinaio

They usually came in small groups setting out on foot together. In Scotland there is a relatively large presence of Barghigiani in Paisley and Glasgow. They brought their moulds with them and depending on where they settled, Garibaldi could become a figure known to the nation: Gladstone in Britain, St Patrick in Ireland. In the Inverness Burgh Directory of 1887–88, there is listed a *Stucco Figure Maker*: Joseph Bernardini of Brown Street. The romanticising of the Jacobite rebellion in the 19th century may well have inspired him to create idealistic figurines of Bonnie Prince Charlie.

Renzo Serafini's father, Luigi, was one of the figurinai who came to Britain at the age of twelve walking with his brother practically all the way across France.

11. Ness Café Window Display (Chocolate Boxes)

Some of the men who remained in Italy were employed in the making of mock chocolates for Cadbury's window display boxes.

One of these workers. Patrizio (Pat) Lunardi, who came to settle in Inverness had memories to tell: how the plaster of Paris would stick in the mens' throats so badly that to keep the saliva flowing they were given a daily allowance of an ounce of Black Twist tobacco to chew.

The explosion in numbers of migrants reached its peak in 1913. The recently-united Kingdom of Italy was not kind to its smallholders. The high levels of taxation were crippling the impoverished peasantry and reports of the wealth of industrialised Britain stirred the imagination. Stories that the streets there were 'paved with gold' did not sound too far-fetched for those who were anxious to believe them.

The route into the UK was through Little Italy in London: the densely-populated and slum-ridden area around Clerkenwell Road, made famous by Charles Dickens in his novel 'Oliver Twist'. There was so much overcrowding in the tenements of Saffron Hill that it became known as 'the Rookery.' There the streets were crowded with street musicians apart from the organ grinders. Amongst them were children who played accordians, concertinas and other instruments, at the same time as others were forced to beg. This exploitation was eventually limited by the passing of the Children Protection Act in 1889.

From London the immigrants spread throughout the country, the Emiliani—those who came from the Parma area (I Parmigiani)— heading to the far North, others West to Wales. The journey north was uninterrupted until they reached Perth, Dundee and more particularly, Aberdeen—as well as Stonehaven and Fraserburgh.

12. Licking Glasses—Ice Cream

CHAPTER FIVE

Trade and Settlement

The immigrants from Val di Taro, the Garfagnana, Lunigiana and Val Magra were from chestnut growing areas and when they left their villages they took with them the only product with which they could trade. In the mid 19th century, when the autumn harvest was ready the *padroni* had consignments of chestnuts sent over. Throughout the winter the smoke and smell of roasted chestnuts would fill the London air as Italians set up barrows and braziers at street corners.

In summer, the ever-enterprising padroni boosted their business by replacing chestnuts with ice-cream.

The making of ice-cream was a time-consuming task, done mostly by small family businesses. In the 19th century there were no ready-mixes, no freezers: it was all prepared in the domestic kitchen where milk was boiled and left to cool overnight. In the morning it was poured into zinc pails, then placed in wooden barrels containing a mixture of ice and salt. When frozen, the ice-cream was taken round the streets in barrows, many of them artistically hand-painted.

Penny ices started to be sold in the late 19th century, not in cones or wafers, but in little glasses called 'licking glasses'. In some parts the sellers were known as the Hokey-Pokey men: a nickname which is believed to have come from their constant cry as they handed over the ices—'ecco un poco' (here's a little!), or 'o che poco' (oh, how little), referring to the cheap price. The custom of using the so-called 'licking glasses' was not very hygienic. Customers would lick the ice cream from the dish which would then be handed back to the vendor who would rinse it before filling it again for the next buyer. Were the glasses adequately washed? Almost certainly not. However, about 1905 the 'ice biscuit' appeared, later to become the cone and the wafer.

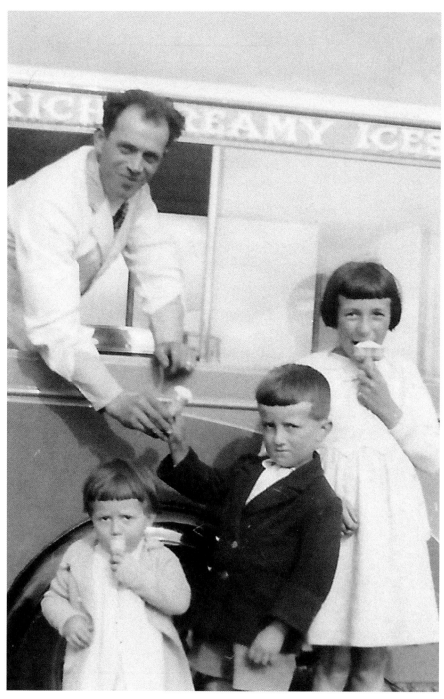

13. *Enrico Pagliari with Leonella Renato Gloria*

CHAPTER SIX

Independent Self-Employed Businesses

By the end of the 19th century people who had been brought over by the padroni or had come to join established family members were beginning to settle down. This was reinforced by the passing of the Aliens Act of 1905 which was to remove the possibility of being an itinerant trader. And so the Italians were forced into a more formal type of trade, giving rise to independent family-based businesses. Thus the old padrone system died out.

The Parmigiani (Italians from the province of Parma) coming into Scotland became independent traders. Not all Scots were happy about this. As Murdoch Rodgers stated in the 1981 *BBC Scotland Odyssey* programme on the early Italians in Scotland:

'In spite of the difficulties which confronted them, some of the pioneer Italians did extremely well. Leopold Giuliani from the village of Barga is said to have owned over sixty cafés in Scotland. By 1914 the 'Ice Cream Parlour' had become a common feature in most towns and villages in Scotland, for the ice-cream cone, like a drink or a flutter, transcended class differences and was enjoyed by rich and poor alike. There were, however, some sections of the local population who looked upon the growth in the trade of ice-cream and its Italian associations with considerable misgivings.'

In today's world of Sunday opening it is hard to understand the hostility the Italians faced when they opened their shop doors on the Sabbath, thus providing the local community with a service no-one else was prepared to offer. After all, in Inverness, even the swings in Bellfield Park were locked up on a Sunday! The townspeople led a fairly strict Presbyterian way of life. So imagine what it was like having been a Roman Catholic Italian at that time! For Italian shop-keepers it was the most stressful day of the week—and one I most dreaded. It was difficult to understand why my friends were at home enjoying a day of family life with their fathers relaxing and playing with them, whilst I had to spend the day sitting out of sight behind the counter, always careful not to get in the way.

As all newsagents were closed on Sundays, the cafés stepped in to fill the gap. For my father, Sunday morning was always a bit of a nightmare. The papers would arrive with the early London train and he had to go down to the station to collect them. Then dozens of orders had to be made up, folded and displayed on the counter in alphabetical order for easy identification—*The News of the World* carefully hidden away in the middle of the order. After church the mad rush would begin: men in their 'Sunday best', women in their obligatory hats. Queues formed as papers, sweets and cartons of ice-cream for the Sunday lunch table were quickly served to prominent members of the bourgeoisie. My father was secretly amused to see many of them tuck the newspapers furtively into their double-breasted overcoats!

However, others were not amused. Strong objection was taken by the United Free Church to Italians opening their shops on Sundays. The claim was that moral as well as spiritual values were under threat.

It was put to a parliamentary Committee on Sunday Trading in 1906 there was the possibility that ice-cream parlours were *morally contaminating.*

> '...as young people of both sexes congregate there after legitimate hours and sometimes misbehave themselves...that is the one great attraction of the ice-cream shops and not the ingredient itself'

The police gave support in claiming that standards of behaviour in ice-cream shops were low and *'acceptable only to their alien owners and to people of loose moral habits'*

The blinkered views of 1920s/30s did not yet focus on the needs of restive adolescents; did not understand that young people wanted to escape from imposed, adult restrictions. And what was the type of beverage these ice-cream shops were selling to their customers? Ice-cream, lemonade, tea, hot chocolate, white coffee, black coffee. No beer, no spirits.

That young men and women of the town were enjoying themselves in places where the strongest drink served was a cup of black coffee was not taken into account. What mattered was 'they were breaking the Sabbath.' That they were sitting in tea-rooms filled with clouds of dense tobacco smoke was not an issue! After all, what man didn't smoke then?

In Inverness, according to Slater's Directory of 1911, we find several of these morally contaminating establishments. Amongst them were: Morganti in Wells Street and Church Street; Donati & Co. in Bridge Street and Eastgate and at no.4 Eastgate, John Coffrini. Giovanni Coffrini (my late brother-in-law's grandfather), from Borgo Val di Taro, was one of the first to open up a chain of Washington Soda Fountains in the North of Scotland. He it was who, directly or indirectly, brought over from his village many of the Italians who eventually opened businesses in Inverness e.g. Giuseppe Bonici who later established himself in Elgin. His son, Albert, first brought the Beatles to the North and was the developer of the Eight Acres Hotel; the two Pizzamiglio brothers, Enrico and Abramo (Antonino), who had businesses in Eastgate; Pietro Ferrari (my father), who came from Aberdeen to take a lease from Angelo Canessa of the Ren-

14. *Washington Soda Fountain*

dezvous café in 1936; Luigi Piscina (my uncle), whose family ran the Ness Café during the second World War; Romola Donati from Castelnuovo, near Barga. Others who came from that area included: Candellini, Bergamini, Lunardi, Turriani (Dorando); Bernardi; Pieraccini.

Enrico (Henry) Turriani told me how his father Renato had come to Inverness before World War I from Riana, a small village near Barga in Tuscany, to work for the Bergamini family. A relaxed, slow-walker, Renato would stroll along the streets of the town and always arrive late for work. The Bergaminis were used to his ways and made fun of him by calling out, *'Come on, Dorando! You're late... hurry up, Dorando!'* This was the name of Dorando Pietri, the Italian marathon runner, who was disqualified after he collapsed and had to be helped over the finishing line at the 1908 Olympics in London. The nickname stuck. Renato was called up to serve in the Italian army and was wounded fighting the Austrians in World War One. He returned to Inverness and opened a café in Church Street which he called *Dorando's*. This was later taken over by his younger son, Bianco, while Henry took over the Academy Street business.

15. Dorando's Café

CHAPTER SEVEN

First World War and its Aftermath

With the outbreak of war in 1914, immigration stopped. Italy joined the Allies in 1915 and immigrants, like Renato Turriani, served in the Italian army. But there was a warning sign of things to come. The Arrotini—the knife-grinders—came from Val Rendena. This was in the Austro-Hungarian Empire, so they were classified as Enemy Aliens and interned, although not for very long. But the stamp of Internment had been used.

At the end of the war, immigration continued but the numbers were decreasing. The established immigrants were sending over to their home towns for others to come and share in the hope of making a better life for themselves.

My father, Pietro Ferrari, was part of this chain. He came to Aberdeen in 1922 to 'help out' in one of the shops run by his brother-in-law, Emilio Bonici.

He had to comply with the Aliens Order that had been passed in 1920. This restricted entry to Britain and required immigrants to have a Work Permit, the granting of which was discretionary. In the Italian community, where people were self-employed, relatives were allowed to come and help in the family business, some as domestic servants. In my mother's document, we see that Aliens had to 'report to the Police on change of residence and on arrival in a new district'.

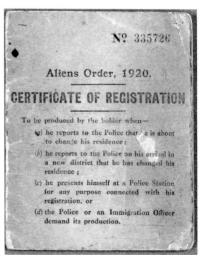

16. Certificate of Registration

My father's passport was issued:

17. *Pietro Ferrari's Passport*

> *In nome di sua maiestà Vittorio Emanuele III per grazia di Dio*
> *volontà della nazione re d'Italia* (In the name of his Majesty
> Victor Emanuel III by the grace of God King of Italy)

So Pietro arrived in Scotland as an Alien, and, as such was carefully
controlled.

What did this young immigrant, typical of many at that time,
leave behind? He left behind not only his wife and baby son, but a
close-knit society which he understood and a culture he probably only
half understood. Near his mountain town, Borgo Val di Taro, is to be
found the beauty and elegance of a Romanesque Italian city: Parma.

From this region of art and music came Giuseppe Verdi, a composer whose early operas express the anguish and heartbreak of those who have to leave their homeland. One only has to listen to the aria, '*Va' pensiero*' from *Nabucco* to feel the initial heartbreak experienced by immigrants all over the world.

My father, faced with language difficulties,—and in Aberdeen the Doric must have presented an even greater problem—the indifference of a people to its new immigrants and the relentless, biting wind of the North-East, decided to go back to the land he knew. However, he reckoned without the toughness of a mountain people used to facing hardships. When he appeared back unexpectedly, his father, a small and resolute man, stared grimly at him. Slowly he pointed to the door and said impassively,

> '*Fuori da qui, non sei figlio mio.*'
> (Out of here, you're no son of mine)

So Pietro went back to Scotland, followed after a year by my mother and their baby son, Bruno.

18. Pietro & Linda Ferrari

This demonstrates to perfection the effect of Chain Migration. He came over to work for his sister-in-law's husband, whose family was well established in Aberdeen since the beginning of the 20th century. After my mother joined him, another of my mother's sisters with her husband arrived, all of whom settled in Scotland. Families from a small town in the Appenines—Pontremoli, near la Spezia (my mother

19. Verdi Monument—Parma

20. Chain Migration

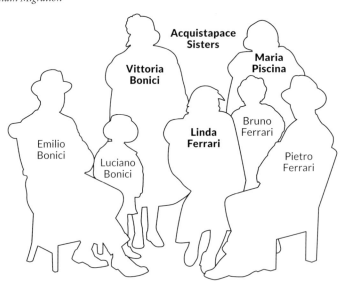

ABERDEEN'S ITALIAN COMMUNITY turned out yesterday to the funeral from St Mary's Cathedral of little Bruno Ferrari, who died in the City Hospital.

24th Nov. 1930.

21. Bruno's Funeral In Aberdeen

had worked there in her youth)—are still resident in Elgin, Stornoway, Nairn & Banff.

This was also a time of great personal grief for my parents: a time when diphtheria was the dread illness, every mother's nightmare. At the age of nine my brother, Bruno, contracted the disease for the second time. Too late, he was taken to the Fever Ward of the City Hospital in Aberdeen.

The entire Italian community turned out for his funeral, demonstrating its solidarity with one of its own in a period of deep sorrow. Aberdonians were able to empathise with their new immigrants as they watched the men processing with the coffin through the streets of the city—the huge wreaths, customary in Italy, causing quite a stir.

My mother, Linda, was overwrought. For a year she visited the cemetery every day before deciding her son should be buried in the land where he had been born. Exhuming a body and transporting it abroad was no easy task. Time and time again permission was refused. In desperation, she wrote a letter to Mussolini, begging him to allow her take her son back to Italy. I still have the draft of that letter.

Her pleading was successful and just over a year later Bruno's body was taken to Borgo Val di Taro where another Funeral Service was held. He is buried in the peaceful cemetery overlooking the valley; the magnificent sculpture erected over his grave is acknowledged to be the most artistic in the area.

22. Bruno's Statue—In Borgo Val Di Taro

That Linda wanted to take her son back to Italy shows the link with the fatherland was then still all-important. Many years later, she told me that she regretted the decision and wished she had left Bruno in Scotland, the land which she now felt was home: a wonderful example of how over the years the first generation Italains had put down their roots.

This was the 1930s when every small town in Scotland had at least one Italian café/ice-cream shop. My father left Aberdeen in 1936 to lease the Rendezvous Café in Inverness until he could afford to open a new business of his own, the Ness Café.

Coming to the small town that was Inverness at that time came as a relief to my parents. They felt more at home here than they had done in Aberdeen; the narrow streets, the old buildings, the faces soon to become familiar. Memories of their relaxed childhood in a similar community flooded back and helped to assuage the pain of losing their first-born.

They arrived in a town that had made room for an astonishing number of Italian immigrants. By 1938/39, in terms of the Inverness Burgh Valuation Roll, there were 20 Italian families with 23 or 24 businesses listed as fruiterer, confectioner, restaurateur, hairdresser and tailor.

The café and the chip shop were now a facet of everyday life. The 'Tally' community was becoming accepted. Families gave their personal service and their special products. In particular, when it came to ice-cream, they had their own original recipes which used fresh milk and other dairy products, such as cream, butter and eggs. Pails of boiled milk would be left to cool on the counter after closing time—so working hours could extend well past midnight. No matter! For amongst the families there was great competition as to whose was the best Ice-Cream in town! After all, they had a great tradition to live up to, going back to the thirteenth century when Marco Polo returned from the East with a recipe that closely resembles today's sherbets and ice creams.

Not all Italians were pleased at the immigrants' success in producing ice-cream. During World War II the US army began making piles of it near the front lines. The belief was that the troops' morale would be boosted by seeing and eating the sweet they associated with home-life. Not to be outdone, the US Navy then built several floating ice-cream 'factories' to keep their men happy.

Mussolini took exception to this. He decided that ice-cream was too much of an American idea and banned the sale of the product throughout Italy. He blamed the Italian people for his fall from power in 1943 and accused them of being a *'mediocre race of good-for-nothings only capable of singing and eating ice-cream.'* How to make friends and influence your own people!

My parents reaction to this condemnation remains a secret.

I was very young at this time and remember very little about family life, except that I rarely saw my father. Only on a Monday—closing day—was he at home. Every other day he would leave the house before we were up and came home long after we had been put to bed. His was a routine of long hours, the shop being open from 7.30am–11.00pm every day, except Mondays and Christmas Day. The

only memory of the family relaxing was that of leisurely meals on closing days, when relatives or friends would turn up. So the men worked
in the shop and sometimes played cards with their compatriots; the
women looked after the children and prepared Italian food at home.
Both men and women, however, followed with keen interest what was
going on back in *la Patria*.

　　And what was going on?

23. Rendezvous Café

CHAPTER EIGHT

The Rise of Fascism

In Italy in the 1920's and 1930's Fascism rose and developed. The immigrants who had come to Britain kept contact with Italy through their families. Like all emigrants they had a great love of the land they called their own. They had kept up their own customs, their own language, their own way of life. The food they ate was not what was served in their shops—there they catered for the British taste of the time. Cooking at home was *all'italiana*. This piece of information was kept secret by the young like me, for no-one wanted to reveal the fact that the food we ate was laced with garlic and olive oil! Olive oil was for babies bottoms—and bought from the chemist!

24. *Mussolini*

For our parents the expectation was that they would go back to Italy in their old age. This hope was fanned by a great sense of nostalgia, successfully tapped by the Fascist Party. Cleverly, the Party courted immigrants, gave them status—they had very little of that in the class-ridden society of the Thirties—and increased their sense of still belonging to Italy.

When Mussolini invaded Abyssinia in October 1935 without a declaration of war, much of his propaganda was directed at Italy's overseas citizens.

25. *Mussolini's Speech On Scarf*

They were the ones who had 'made it'; whom he could induce to help out la patria. Funds were needed for the war and so, cleverly, modest demands were made of the women in particular. After all, very few could donate cash, but every married woman had a wedding-ring: a gold one. These rings were handed over to the Party and a replacement ring of steel was handed out. On them was inscribed *Oro alla Patria* (gold for the fatherland) with the date *18-11-35-XIV*—the date being the day when economic sanctions were imposed on Italy by 50 States of the League of Nations and the Roman numeral indicating the 14th year of the Fascist era. In Italy women queued up to hand over their rings, motivated by the example of Queen Elena who performed the first symbolised act of Italy's 'wedding ring day' before the tomb of the Unknown Soldier.

General Badoglio's subsequent march into Addis Ababa in May 1936 was trumpeted with pride by the Fascist regime; silk mustard-coloured scarves printed with Mussolini's speech of triumph were bought and worn by female immigrants in Britain. Fascism was playing on the strong feeling of patriotism.

Clubs had opened up in the major cities, known as the 'Fascio'. For most Italians in Scotland they represented an opportunity to lead a limited social life. It was especially important to the women who had few occasions to meet up with those who spoke their own language. Here they gathered for dances, receptions and concerts. One could compare them to the clubs of the Scots abroad where the feeling of nostalgia takes over from everyday reality. Think of the importance of St Andrew's Night to Scots overseas! There was, however, a political input in the 'Fascio' clubs and there were certainly members who were dyed-in-the-wool supporters of Mussolini. I vaguely remember my father referring to any man he seemed to dislike as, '*quel brutto Fascista!*' (that horrible Fascist).

In Inverness there was no Fascio, the nearest being in Aberdeen. Here, being geographically isolated, families in the North of Scotland could not and did not have the collective impact of the large number of immigrants in the big cities. They were simply not involved in political affairs. There was, however, a continuing sense of nostalgia and patriotism. One had only to see the sadness in my mother's face when she spoke of the loved ones whom she had not seen in years.

CHAPTER NINE

The Threat of War

The British Government was understandably concerned with the build-up of Fascism. There was a growing discussion as to how the Italian Community was to be dealt with in the event of Mussolini coming into the war. Ominous signs of trouble ahead came with the signing of the Pact of Steel on 22 May 1939—a military and political alliance between the Kingdom of Italy and Germany.

Understandably, public opinion was turning against the Italian community and, in particular, an article in the *Daily Mirror* on 26 April 1940—almost two months before Italy declared war—demonstrates how xenophobia against Italians was building up:

> 'There are more than twenty thousand Italians in Great Britain. London alone shelters more than eleven thousand of them. The London Italian is an indigestible unit of population... And so the boats unload all kinds of brown-eyed Francescas and Marias, beetle-browed Ginos, Titos and Marios...'

The reporter excels in his imagery:

> 'Now every Italian colony in Great Britain and America is a seething cauldron of smoking Italian politics. Black fascism. Hot as hell. Even the peaceful, law-abiding proprietor of the back-street coffee shop bounces into a fine patriotic frenzy at the sound of Mussolini's name...'

This probably led to a question being put in the House of Commons on May 30 1940, urging that the Home Secretary,

> '...in the interest of public safety, have an inquiry made into the Savoy Hotel which is staffed with anti-British Italians, seeing that highly-placed officers frequently dine there.'

In Inverness, on 18 May 1940, the *Highland News* ran the headline:

'*Curfew on Italians'—the position at Inverness*
It continued: ' the Home Office has ordered all male aliens, of whatever nationality, over the age of 16 and under the age of 60 to be subject to the following restrictions:
> 1. They shall report daily in person to a police station.
> 2. They shall not make use of any motor vehicles (other than a public conveyance), or any bicycle: and
> 3. They shall not be out of doors between the hours of 8.00pm and 6.00am.'

Curfew on Italians

THE POSITION AT INVERNESS|

26. *Curfew On Italians*

Considering the opening hours of most Italian businesses in the town, the last restriction meant that most of the men had to sleep in their business premises. Of the twenty-one Italian shopkeepers in Inverness, very few were naturalised British subjects.

I now understand why my father no longer seemed to be around and why there was always a strange tense atmosphere in the house. The grown-ups were less tolerant with the young; high-spirited behaviour being frowned upon and plainly discouraged. Laughter disappeared as anxiety increased.

The first restriction led to a conviction of two Italians, reported in the *Northern Chronicle*, 29 May 1940. The two Pizzamiglio brothers of Eastgate (Enrico and Antonino) were fined the sum of £10 for failing to report to a police office on the previous Sunday;

> 'The excuse put forward by both the accused was that they had been very busy on this particular day and it was not until after 8.00pm that they remembered about reporting, and if they left their homes at that time in the evening, they would have been committing another offence.'

The restrictions on men who had been in Scotland for almost twenty years were bad enough, but worse was to follow.

CHAPTER TEN

Mussolini Declares War

On Mussolini's declaration of War on 10 June 1940, my older sister, Gloria, told me of my mother's sudden scream and immediate reaction:

'Ormai ci siamo—o Dio, abbia pieta di noi!'
(Now we're for it—Oh God, have pity on us!).

THE INVERNESS COURIER, TUESDAY

ITALY DECLARES WAR

MUSSOLINI FULFILS PROMISE TO HITLER

27. Italy Declares War

Overnight from Aliens we had all become Enemy Aliens.

War is not a time of tolerance. With the fall of France imminent and fear of Fifth Colomnists rife in Britain, Churchill's immediate response was *Collar the lot!*

The declaration of war was announced on the 6 o' clock News. After 10.00pm hundreds of Italians all over Scotland were arrested. The anguish of families was heightened by the darkness of the black-out, a time when even irrational fears take over from reality.

In Inverness some men were taken to the Police Cells in Castle Wynd, others to Porterfield Prison.

Along with the sudden confusion, mistakes were made. All those with Italian names were suspect, no matter the land of their birth. Enrico Pagliari, who ran a Fish & Chip restaurant in Academy Street, was arrested along with the others. He was first imprisoned then sent to the Isle of Man. It was later discovered he had been born in France and was, therefore, a citizen of one of Britain's closest allies. When informed that he could return home to Inverness, he was none too pleased at having to leave before his friends.

Being born in Scotland did not automatically protect the men from interment.

Loreto Celli, a tailor in Inverness, was arrested with his sixteen year old son, Ottavio (Tavio). They were both held in a cell in Castle Wynd for two days before being transferred to Porterfield Prison. Despite his young age and being born in Glasgow, Tavio was held under Defence Regulation 18B as being a threat to National Security. This regulation allowed the government to act immediately if there was any doubt as to a person's loyalty in time of war. Many young men of Italian origin suffered the same fate. There was no time to pack a case—Tavio was out with a friend when he heard the news. For two days he and his father were held in solitary confinement until things calmed down.

Another seventeen year old Invernessian, Enrico Turriani, remembers the chain of events;

> 'Suddenly from being Aliens we had become Enemy Aliens. We all waited for the blow to fall. At 2.00am on 11 June the dreaded knock at the door came. An Inspector and a Special Constable were standing there, looking rather embarrassed—after all, we all knew one another. We were told that my father and I were being arrested, that we could take a few clothes with us. My younger brother was under sixteen at the time, so he was left to comfort my mother, who felt the world collapsing around her.'

Renzo Serafini, born in Hawick, who had come to Inverness in 1932 with his parents, brother and sister, recalled;

> 'Er, that night. The 10th June. We heard the news, whatever time it was. So I shut the shop and came down and I said to my mother, "I'm going up to pack my cases." "Oh" my father says, "Don't be daft. Don't worry." I says, "My brother and I will be off tomorrow. They'll come for us." So they shut the shop

about ten o'clock. About one o'clock a big knock at the door: the Chief of Police. "I've always wanted to do this—with one of the business people of the town." So he said. He was with a friend of mine who was a policeman... he got him to come and arrest me. The Chief says, "Right, Archie..." "Oh no!" says Archie, "not Renzo." "Yes." says the Chief, "You're coming with me." So Archie started crying when he seen me. "Renzo" he says. "Honest, I didn't want to come. *That bastard...*he wanted it..." So they took me and then said, "And your father..." My sister rebelled. "My father, no!" She went over and hit the Chief of Police: "You're not taking my father!" He gave her a push, she came back and hit him...But my father had to come along. He was over a year interned.'

Renzo, at that time, was a supporter of Mussolini and very out-spoken. His room was searched before he was led away with his father, Luigi, and his younger brother Vittorio (Vic). Only Renzo was made to take off his shoes and belt before leaving for the police station at Castle Wynd.

My cousin, Luciano Bonici, was fifteen years old when his father, Emilio, was arrested. Luciano's daughter, Paola, tells of what happened on the night of 10 June in Aberdeen:

'Two policemen came to the door of the house late in the evening. One of them searched the house for subversive materials, before going to the shop to arrest nonno (grand-dad). As the Detective Inspector knew nonno well, he was embarrassed by the situation and insisted they walk down the street as though taking a stroll. No word of where they were going was said, no time to take any clothes was given—not even a pair of pyjamas. Nonno was taken to Craig Inshes Prison where he joined all the other Italian nationals rounded up that night. There he met one of his friends who had been picked up during the day at the dog-racing and taken straight to prison without anyone informing his family.'

My father was taken away while I slept.

The *Northern Chronicle's* leader of 12 June 1940 was uncompromising;

The Stab in the Back

'Mussolini has joined his fellow gangster Hitler in the latter's war against Christian civilisation…It is the act of an assassin, and has earned for him in the Press of the world the epithets of 'murderer', 'thug', 'jackal'…

One thing is certain: whatever the outcome of the war Mussolini's name will go down to history as that of a villain of the first order, a man who stabbed in the back in their hour of peril the nations to whom his country owes its very existence. It was Garibaldi, the great Italian patriot, who called down a curse on his country if it ever drew the sword against Britain. The curse is likely to be fulfilled.'

It is not surprising that the Italian community in Inverness was in a state of sheer panic. Suddenly, men were removed from their families, their homes, their businesses. For almost a week they were held in police cells or Porterfield prison, their relations receiving no information as to their whereabouts, although in a small town, the secrecy was pointless.

Round-Up of Local Italians

MAJORITY OF SHOPS RE-OPEN

28. Round-up

The *Highland News* of 15 June 1940, in the article **Round-Up of Local Italians**, writes that there were hostile demonstrations in the east and west of Scotland. But in Inverness the round-up was uneventful in this respect. The reporter even found an amusing side to it all:

'One Italian evidently saw no reason why he should not enjoy at least a modicum of home comfort if he was to be detained. He arrived in the police patrol car in the Castle Street parking stance, taken into custody, and returned a few minutes later to the car, and emerged with a comfortable-looking armchair resting on his head and shoulders.'

There was, however, a serious side for the families which came out when a local official was asked how the businesses would function without their owners:

> 'Off-hand I should not like to offer an opinion as to the appropriate procedure to be followed with regard to the businesses of Italians. I therefore cannot definitely state into whose hands the drawings from such shops will now go. One thing is absolutely certain—not a penny will go to the enemy.'

Just before Italy entered the war, my first recollection of the time was one of bewilderment. It was the day a workman came to dismantle our wireless, Aliens not being allowed to possess a radio for fear of news being transmitted to the enemy. I was in the kitchen playing with my brother, Renato. Very curious as to what was happening, I bombarded the man with questions. He ignored them all, his face hard and fixed. After he had opened the back of the radio, I ran over and bent down to look inside. Disappointed, I turned to Renato and asked, 'Oh, no! What's happened? Where have all the little people gone?' My brother, a good three years older, snapped back scornfully, 'Don't be so stupid!' For the first time the workman looked at me.

His expression softened and he smiled.

The leader in the *Highland News* of 15 June 1940, seems to have come up with a solution to the problem of how the Italian businesses would function without their proprietors:

> 'The whole position with regard to the Italian shops and the stocks they contain seems to be obscure at the moment but it is suggested that the most feasible solution of the difficulty would be to realise the value of the stocks and devote the proceeds to the maintenance of the internees, leaving the British proprietors of such premises to make whatever use of their property they might think fit.
>
> Such an arrangement would operate hardly in the case of Italian shopkeepers of long standing and with strong affiliations in this country but they would simply be obliged to regard it as the fortune, or rather the misfortune of war.'

As it turned out, businesses were left in the hands of employees or closed down, In Inverness not even the wives were to be left in charge for they had the disadvantage of living in a town on the coast next to an area which had been declared under the Defence Regulations to be a Protected Area covering the North of Scotland. With large concentrations of military forces and important bases in the area, no person was allowed to enter or leave without showing an ID card and a permit. The Commando Memorial at Spean Bridge is a reminder of the intense and often secret training of this time.

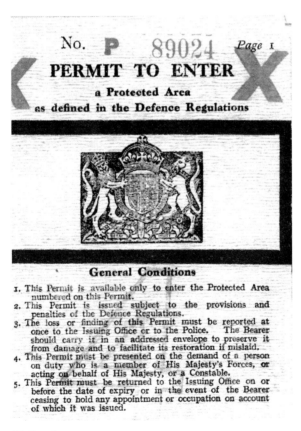

General Conditions

1. This Permit is available only to enter the Protected Area numbered on this Permit.
2. This Permit is issued subject to the provisions and penalties of the Defence Regulations.
3. The loss or finding of this Permit must be reported at once to the Issuing Office or to the Police. The Bearer should carry it in an addressed envelope to preserve it from damage and to facilitate its restoration if mislaid.
4. This Permit must be presented on the demand of a person on duty who is a member of His Majesty's Forces, or acting on behalf of His Majesty, or a Constable.
5. This Permit must be returned to the Issuing Office on or before the date of expiry or in the event of the Bearer ceasing to hold any appointment or occupation on account of which it was issued.

29. Permit

CHAPTER ELEVEN

Women Relocated

But for Alien women not even a permit protected them or their young families. By the 1940 Aliens (Protected Areas) (No.5) Order they were ordered to leave Inverness and reside at least twenty miles away from the coast. The relocation of women in the Highlands is a factor that has been glossed over by many writers of this period—perhaps, because it did not happen in the more populated areas of Scotland. Within twelve days the Italian women in Inverness witnessed their husbands and sons imprisoned, saw their businesses left without direction, understood that their homes were no longer places of refuge.

The *Highland News* of 22 June 1940 tells its readers:

> 'The women-folk will have their temporary home in a delightful spot high amid the hills'.

The *'temporary home'* was accommodation in hotels, boarding-houses or with private families, depending on what each family could afford to pay because no official provision had been made for accommodation. The *'delightful spot'* turned out to be Tomintoul the highest village and one of the most remote in the Highlands. The reporter writes that there was a 'paternal touch' when one police officer said to a little girl, 'See and come back with roses in your cheeks'.

One can imagine the feelings of the women as they travelled by bus from their homes into the hills of what was then a very remote village where they had to register. A few brought with them blankets, shawls and pillows in case they had to sleep in the open. They arrived in Tomintoul at nine in the evening, a time of deepening shadows and increasing apprehension.

30. Teresa Gatti's Registration Certificate

31. Teresa Gatti Reporting at Tomintoul

Again, the great Dante expresses the moments of despair:

> *Nessun maggior dolore,*
> *Che ricordarsi del tempo felice*
> *Nella miseria*
> (There is no greater sorrow than to recall a time of happiness in misery.) *Inferno v*

The womens' difficulty in finding their own accommodation was eased when the local priest, Father Auer, stepped in to help them. As it turned out, many of the Italian women found Tomintoul a quiet and soothing place, its peaceful atmosphere and its little Church of Our Lady of Saint Michael's reminding them of the villages and churches of their childhood. At that time Tomintoul was a village with no gas, no electricity, but to them the paraffin lamps and open fires were of comfort.

32. *St Michael's Tomintoul*

Many businesses had to be entrusted to employees and it is a credit to Inverness that there were no anti-Italian riots in the town—unlike the capital of Scotland where some of the worst scenes occurred. The men having been arrested, it was the women and children in the Central Belt who were subjected to the terror of mobs on the rampage.

The *Evening News* reported on 11 June 1940:

> 'Leith Street and Leith Walk looked in places as if a series of heavy bombs had fallen. In Italian premises not a scrap of glass remained in single or double windows, furniture broken, window frames and dressing destroyed and the cigarette machines at the entrances damaged beyond repair.'

Alien mother stays to nurse son

MRS LINDA FERRARI who has already given two blood transfusions to her two-year-old boy Francisco, ill in Inverness Hospital, has been reprieved from the east coast ban on aliens.

The boy, suffering from anæmia, has been ill since March, when he received four blood transfusions, two from his father and two from his mother.

Hearing that the Ferrari family had been ordered to leave the doctor called on Saturday, and after testing their son's blood he ordered him back to the infirmary, telling Mrs Ferrari she would need to give more transfusions.

Pietro Ferrari, the father, who had a restaurant at I Ness Walk, Inverness, is now interned.

"I am so thankful to be allowed to stay near my baby," said Mrs Ferrari. "I do not know how long I am to be permitted to stay in Inverness, but I think it is until baby is better."

33. *Alien Mother*

CHAPTER TWELVE

The Compassion of Inverness

And how did the citizens of the Inverness area react to these measures? Here there was no open antagonism; perhaps more a general feeling of passive sympathy. The knowledge that men were being sent away—as yet no-one knew where—and women were being bussed to an unspecified destination aroused the compassion of some local families who offered to look after the very young.

My mother's plight was desperate. Her husband was imprisoned, her two-year old son was critically ill in hospital in need of blood transfusions, she had a business to run and, on top of it all, she was expected to leave Inverness for Tomintoul. In her time of most need she was aided by two kind-hearted 'pillars of the community'.

One was the Honorary Charge Physician of the Royal Northern Infirmary, Dr Duncan Leys, who fought tooth and nail for her to stay in Inverness to give the necessary transfusions to her sick child.

Her dilemma was picked up by the press with the headline:

Alien mother stays to nurse son.
Mrs Linda Ferrari has already given two blood transfusions to her two-year-old boy Francesco, ill in Inverness Hospital, has been reprieved from the east coast ban on aliens.

The boy, suffering from anaemia, has been ill since March, when he received four blood transfusions, two from his father and two from his mother.

Hearing that the Ferrari family had been ordered to leave, the doctor called on Saturday, and after testing their son's blood he ordered him back to the infirmary, telling Mrs Ferrari she would need to give more transfusions.

Pietro Ferrari, the father, who had a restaurant at 1 Ness

Walk, Inverness, is now interned.

'I am so thankful to be allowed to stay near my baby,' said Mrs Ferrari. 'I do not know how long I am to be permitted to stay in Inverness, but I think it is until my baby is better'.

Sadly, Francesco died fourteen days after Mussolini entered the war.

The other Invernessian to whom my mother was forever grateful was Police Inspector Alistair Chisholm, a man whose sense of compassion triumphed over the need to further his career. At this time of wretchedness he and his family took my brother and me into his home and care. When asked by a Superior if he realised he was putting his prospect of promotion at risk by taking in Alien children, his reaction was swift; the children needed protecting, they were under his protection and he would make sure that they were protected.

34. *Bellfield Park – tennis courts*

Of this troubled period most of what I remember are images of kind faces and sounds of tennis balls at Bellfield Park thudding in the calm June evenings as I looked down from my unfamiliar bedroom window. Also, there is a faint recollection of confusion when I saw my older brother, Renato, crying: unlike me, he was just old enough to have a vague understanding of death.

As Francesco was dying other issues were making the headlines. The *Highland News*, on 22 June 1940 had a column, headed:

'Italian Women Depart—Last Phase in Dispersal.
On the eve of their farewell the women folk visited the Burgh Police Department and had their papers duly checked up. Some of them were not able to see either their fathers or brothers at the place of detention. The farewells on the part of the young people were moving,. The estrangement in some instances has been poignant…'

The reporter writes that those in charge of the Italian businesses were British subjects:

'They are acting under power of attorney to settle up matters or to ensure a continuing of the various shops being conducted always subject to the the restrictions imposed under the Trading With the Enemy Act…this special piece of legislation prevents the 'takings' finding their way into enemy countries.'

THE HIGHLAND NEWS,

Italian Women Depart

LAST PHASE IN DISPERSAL

35. Italian Women Depart

36. *Isle of Man—Prison Camp*

CHAPTER THIRTEEN

Internment

As the women struggled with problems at home, the men were held for approximately three weeks in the Donaldson's Institute for the Deaf in Edinburgh before being shipped to the Isle of Man. Amongst those held there were: the Serafinis, the Giubarellis, the Pizzamiglios, the Pieraccinis, Loreto Celli, Enrico Turriani, Enrico Pagliari, Luigi Piscina.

The men's internment in the Isle of Man was to last, in general, until late 1943. They were the lucky ones. There were others who had been shipped to Canada and Australia for the duration of the war. They, too, were lucky. The unlucky ones were those who perished at the bottom of the sea on July 2, 1940—approximately 446 Italian internees when the ship carrying them to Canada was torpedoed by a German U-boat. For anyone of Italian origin in this country the very name Arandora Star hurts—like a knife in an open wound. But that it is a story in itself.

Enrico Turriani's recollection of the time is forceful:

'It was sheer chance that no-one from the Inverness area was on board the ill-fated ship. The train taking us to the docks of Liverpool was held up for many hours on the way because of a heavy air-raid on the line. We arrived too late for any one to be put on board.'

Gradually the feverish atmosphere gripping Britain in the two months following Mussolini's entry into war started to weaken. The public began to calm down and a more rational view of the predicament facing internees was expressed by Lord Cecil in the House of Lords on 6 August 1940:

> 'I feel most strongly that the history of what has taken place with regard to these unhappy aliens is one of the most discreditable incidents in the whole history of this country'.

This moderate view was taken up in the Commons debate of 22 August by Sir John Anderson:

> 'I am not here to deny for a moment that most regrettable and deplorable things have happened...They have been due partly to the inevitable haste with which the policy of internment, once decided upon, had to be carried out. They have been due in some cases to the mistakes of individuals and to stupidity and muddle.'

37. Porterfield Prison, Inverness

CHAPTER FOURTEEN

War Time

In the meantime, after three months in Tomintoul, the women were allowed to return home. For the first time, since coming to this country the wives of the Italian immigrants were face to face with the British public. It was not an easy undertaking. Up until now, most of them had led a sheltered life either at home looking after the children and cooking, or in the back premises of the shop preparing food and washing dishes. They had been cut off from the customers and as a result had very little English. Suddenly they were catapulted into the running of a business in a hectic wartime situation. It was no time to hide away in the back shop. My mother also had to think of her husband, Pietro, who was not sent to the Isle of Man but kept in Porterfield because of a stomach ulcer that was causing concern. In those days his condition was painful and life-threatening—the ulcer was to cost him his life five years after the war ended. Because of his medical condition and fearful of the diet he would be faced with in prison, my mother made sure that food was delivered to him twice a day. I usually accompanied my sister, Gloria, when she brought his meals up to Porterfield. There, we would ring the bell and wait for a warder to pull back the grill of a small window in the massive door. Young as we both were, there was an instinctive sense of humiliation that our father was a prisoner. My father was last recorded in the Prison Journal on 7 January 1941: Prisoner 120/40.

Meantime the cafés, the chip-shops came into their own, providing a welcome change of diet for an austerity-ridden public. It was a time of ingenuity; a time to find ways of feeding a hungry population, especially troops who were tired of Naafi food.

38. *Ration book recipes*

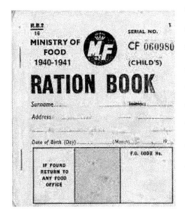

39. *Ration book*

Alongside British troops, were men of many other nationalities who poured into the town; Canadian, American, Australian, Norwegian, Polish. Word got around that a little lady in the Rendezvous Café was serving Sausage and Chips Surprise; a luxury dish where an egg, or maybe two, lay hidden beneath a pile of chips, courtesy of the Egg Grading Station.

My older sister, Gloria, recalled another job she particularly disliked:

'Throughout the war eggs were difficult to come by, and most people hated the dried eggs which had to be reconstituted. Imagine their delight on discovering a fresh egg hidden under a pile of chips on their plate. The Egg Grading staion used to sell broken eggs to the public, so I used to go up to Argyle Street, where I would queue with my pail which would eventually be filled to the brim with floating yolks that stared unblinkingly at me. For years afterwards I couldn't face the sight of an egg!'

In the cafes fights broke out—especially when the Lumberjacks were in town—and some brave members of staff would intervene in an effort to save the shop from being wrecked. One attempt to stop the brawling in the Rendezvous Café resulted in a waitress being knocked unconscious, leaving her with a black eye for weeks. The Military Police, however, were always quick off the mark and that night the soldier involved was uncerimoniously seized and driven away, later to be court-martialled.

Gradually the internees trickled back—to find that the women they had left behind had coped admirably. Renzo Serafini maintained:

'I always said that the women were the heroes of this war for both countries because it's them that kept the shops open'.

Some of the men were released after only six months, provided they did work of National Importance: e.g. farm labourer. In the Inverness area many farmers understood the dilemma facing those who had businesses to run. Nominally they accepted the regulation, hired the Italians and turned a blind eye to their not always turning up for work.

40. *Linda Ferrari & Gloria*

41. Highland Restaurant—Primo Pieraccini

The HIGHLAND RESTAURANT

· · TRY · ·
A CAROLINA SPECIAL 6d
America's Popular Chocolate
Malted Milk

MENU
HIGH TEAS AND SUPPERS

Hot or Cold Drinks

All Kinds of
Flavours

GRILLS AND SAVOURIES

FRIED HADDOCK or FILLET (with Chips)	6d
GRILLED HADDOCK or FILLET (with Chips)	8d
TINNED SALMON (with Chips)	10d
GRILLED STEAK (with Chips)	1/2 and 1/8
GRILLED CHOP (with Chips)	1/2 and 1/8
GRILLED BEEF SAUSAGES (with Chips)	8d
GRILLED PORK SAUSAGES (with Chips)	10d
MIXED GRILL (with Chips)	1/8
CORNED BEEF (with Chips)...	6d
BACON and EGG (with Chips)	1/-
FRIED EGG (with Chips)	6d
HOT MEAT PIE (with Chips)	5d and 6d
WELSH RAREBIT on TOAST	8d
SCRAMBLED EGG on TOAST	6d
BAKED BEANS on TOAST	6d
SARDINES on TOAST	6d
CHEESE TOAST with BACON	8d
CHEESE TOAST	6d
MACARONI with BEEF, TOMATO and CHEESE ...	9d
FRIED CHIPPED POTATOES (Per Portion) ...	2d and 3d
GREEN PEAS (Per Portion)	2d and 3d
BAKED BEANS (Per Portion)	3d and 4d
TOMATOES or SALAD . ... ·	3d

SANDWICHES

SPECIAL " HIGHLAND " SANDWICH	3d
ROAST BEEF or HAM SANDWICH	3d
SARDINES or CHEESE SANDWICH	3d
TOMATO SANDWICH	3d
EGG SANDWICH	6d

BEVERAGES

POT of TEA } For One Person	4d
Freshly made } For Each Additional Person	3d
CUP of TEA .·	2d
COFFEE, Freshly made, Black, or with Cream	4d
COCOA ... ... Plain, 2d; with Milk	3d
BOVRIL or OXO with BISCUIT	4d
HORLICK'S MALTED MILK (Chocolate or Plain) ...	4d
OVALTINE or BOURN-VITA	5d
MILK SHAKES (Any Flavour)	4d
GLASS of MILK	3d
AERATED WATERS (Per Glass)	3d and 4d

SUNDRIES

BREAD and BUTTER (Per Slice)	1d
TOAST (Per Slice)	1½d
CAKES (Each)	1½d
BISCUITS, Plain or Creams (in Packets) ...	1d, 3d and 6d
CHOCOLATE BISCUITS	1d and 2d
CHEESE and BISCUITS (Per Person)	3d
JAM or MARMALADE (Per Person)	2d
ICES, FRUITS, CHOCOLATES, CIGARETTES, Etc., Etc.	

42. Highland Restaurant Menu

CHAPTER FIFTEEN

Post War

The end of the war did not bring with it a relaxation of rationing, indeed, food shortages became even more acute with millions of starving Europeans to feed.

The Italians found that their form of eating establishment was just what the public wanted. Café cuisine was simple, tasty and affordable. It was the era of 'morning coffee' and 'afternoon tea' and—most important—'high tea'. From 4.00pm–11.00pm the public came in droves for the ubiquitous pot of tea, buttered bread, cakes, and the ever-popular mixed grill.

Sausages, bacon, chops, steak, haddock, sole, scrambled, poached and fried eggs, baked beans, sardines(tinned), macaroni and cheese—all covered with the obligatory heap of chips. The back-shop was a hive of activity, a place of stress and, at times, of hilarity. Teresa Gatti, who had come to Inverness in the late 1930s to look after us as young children, was now commandant in the café kitchen and not a woman to be trifled with;

43. *Teresa the Commandant*

It's not fair; my order was in first. The customer's complaining...

...*Tell wait. This no the Ritz.*

Where's my egg?

...*Hen too tired today.*

Is this meant to be Welsh Rarebit?

...*Yes, all'italiana.*

Teresa, there's supposed to be tea in the teapot!

...*No worry! Hot water good for stomach.*

'*O, sole mio, sta fronte a me...*'

Never mind the 'sole', Teresa! Where's my haddock?

Eggs could be found but sweet-rationing hit the confectionery shops hard. The allotted allowance of sweets was minimal so my mother had to think of a way to give her sugar-deprived customers an occasional treat. She did this by making mountains of tablet at home. Always our kitchen table was covered with it and a sugary, sickly smell pervaded the whole house—even today, I cannot bear the sight of it. Cut into squares and carefully wrapped in grease-proof paper it would then be taken to the shop. There it would be hidden under the counter and furtively kept for well-known customers—or for children whose disappointment at the size of their ration was apparent to her.

As old faces reappeared and wounds healed, pre-war Italians found that they had quietly changed. My father was a regular patron of the British Legion whenever he could escape from behind the counter: his service in the Italian Army in World War I allowing him entry to the Legion. Daly Pennington, the electrician, whose business was in Young Street, used to drag him away from the shop with the words, 'Come on, Potato Pete, stop peeling those spuds and get your apron off!' Pietro, thin and gaunt, could not have been less like the character portrayed in the Propaganda posters of the time!

44. *Potato Pete*

Patria was still important to the first generation Italians but so was the land that they—and their children—called their own. Some of their offspring had served in the British Armed Services: Councillor Mario Bernardi served in the RAF; Plavo Bernardi died on 20 July 1940 serving in the Middlesex Regiment: his funeral took place amid the trauma the Italian women were experiencing (an example of the irrationality of war); Victor Bergamini was killed in action; 'Scotty' Bernardi served with the Highland Division at St Valery where he was taken prisoner. He eventually escaped and returned to Scotland. Michael Persichini also served and my cousin,

Gilda Piscina was in the WRAF.

First generation Italians had been shocked by the ordeal they had suddenly experienced during the war and came to a rational conclusion: that they should show allegiance to the country where their roots were now firmly planted. Many sought and gained Naturalisation, as did my parents in 1947.

But what was there in Inverness to entertain its youth in the 1950s? Frequent visits to one of three cinemas—the Playhouse, the La Scala, the Palace. They not only showed the latest blockbusters (e.g Gone with the Wind) but also provided customers with good food in their tea-rooms. The Playhouse was particularly attractive with its early 1930s style. Like a theatre, it had boxes on both sides of the auditorium and at Christmas, the manager, James (Jimmy) Nairn, would transform the interior into an out of this world Disneyland. For me and for other elderly Invernessians the thrill of being taken to see the magical transformation is a memory that never fades. Sadly, the cinema and its decorations perished in the fire of March 1972.

There the nostalgia lies: the carefully-vetted films my mother used to take me to see through the thick haze of cigarette smoke. Vetted the main film may have been but she could not control what unexpected scenes of intimacy might be lurking in the second feature movie. When romantic moments were shown—a lingering kiss at most—she, like some mothers of that era, would hurriedly cover my eyes with her hand. That hand would also protect me from the disinfectant sprayed over cinema-goers by the usherettes as they walked up and down the aisles.

Besides the cinema there were the much-frequented cafés: teas and coffees in the 'Wash', the Washington Soda Fountain, much loved by 'bikers' for its well-used juke-box and further up Eastgate a chat with Rosie in the Mayfair Café—both cafés run by the Pizzamiglio brothers. Across the river opposite the Suspension Bridge, the Rendezvous and the Ness Café competed to serve the young with ice-cream and soft drinks, while fish and chips was the speciality in Serafini's West End 'chipper'. Not to be outdone, 'Ernie's in Academy Street and Pieraccini's Highland Restaurant in Eastgate claimed their fish suppers were the best to be had. Frequenting these and the many other cafés of the town was the high-light of an evening out in the town centre. Local pubs were, of course, closed on Sundays but even during week days they were taboo for girls—only a 'hussy' would dare to be seen there! Nor were girls allowed to patronise Hunter's Billiard Salon—an inflexible male sanction. On a Saturday night for both male and female there was the enjoyment of a dance in the Caledonian ball-room (the Caley). This was, perhaps, as compensation for the rigours of the Sabbath they were about to face: two long Church services, one in the morning and another in the evening, with Sunday school for the very young. A staid walk round the Islands, where my mother ran the Tearoom, was the only exercise allowed on the 'day of rest'. So much for the 'morally contaminating' complaints of 1906!

45. *Charlie's Café—Early 1960s*

The Fifties and Sixties saw changes in the type of eating places the public wanted. Café styles altered. Joe Boni, who had come to Inverness after the war, opened the Castle Restaurant which is still continued by his descendents. A new addition to the café scene was Charlie Pieraccini's café in Farraline Park—its location and juke-box drawing in the bikers.

The transformation of the town itself began at the end of the 50s. Customs and beliefs were changing—'keeping up with the times' as it is said—and buildings became targets for demolition. On 31 August 1959 the suspension bridge whose warm sandstone structure complemented that of the Castle was closed forever to traffic. The bridge that stands today opened on 28 September 1961, a sombre day of heavy rain—in mourning, perhaps—it being the anniversary of the collapse of the main bridge over the Ness in 1664.

Bridge Street and Castle Tolmie were the next offenders in the planners' vision of the future. In 1961 the demolition started of the cobbled street, narrow closes and historic four-storyed tenements in order to erect a concrete-panelled eyesore. Where was the vision? Did no eye see the incongruity of the grey blocks against the pink battlements of the castle?

There were instances of customers crying in the Ness Café as they watched the destruction going on beside the river. I know my mother certainly did.

And it went on and on, down Church

46. New Bridge Construction

Street through to Queensgate where the bulldozers went to work on one of the most imposing Victorian buildings in the town: the old Post Office. Academy Street was not spared when the Empire Theatre hit the dust in 1971, thereby laying the ghosts of Harry Gordon and Dave Willis, comics loved over the years by Invernessians young and old.

Perhaps one of the saddest moments for the townsfolk was the disappearance of the three statues, incorrectly known as the Three Graces (instead of the Three Virtues) 'Faith, Hope and Charity'. All of nine feet in height they once stood above the buildings in the centre looking down with dignity on those entering and leaving the Town Hall. In 1955 their dominance came to an end when Mackay's Clan Tartan & Tweed Warehouse was demolished. For six years the 'Graces' lay unwanted in a Council yard. Then, in 1961, someone remembered them and decided to rid the town of the useless encumbrance they had become. The Town Council announced they were available

47. The Three Graces

to anyone willing to remove them at no cost; as a result they went into exile to Orkney. Forty-six years later the Common Good Fund bought them back for £15,000. Today, the truncated remains stare at the river beside Ness Bank Church, musing on the grandeur that once was theirs.

So Inverness changed and so did those who lived there.

48. *Renzo Serafini—Highland Italian Circle*

In 1967 Renzo Serafini, whose outspoken opinions had kept him interned in the Isle of Man until the end of the war, came to be valued as the affable and fun-loving proprietor of the Locarno Café in Academy Street. He was a founder-member of the Highland Italian Circle, still active today. His view was that even if many who joined the club did not have a knowledge of Italian, they could acquire an understanding of how the love of *Patria* and *Scozia* is intertwined.

The second generation of Italian origin was growing up. It was expected that these young people would carry on the work that their parents had painstakingly started. Some of them had other ideas. To start with, their first language was not Italian. Many of them had only an understanding of what their parents were saying when they spoke in Italian—and the understanding of Italian was practically non-existent if their parents spoke to one another in their local dialect. Then there was the problem of the position in which they had found themselves at the outbreak of war. If it had been a difficult time for the adults who had found themselves enemy aliens, imagine the dilemma of the young who had had to put up with their erstwhile, friendly playmates calling them 'Eye-ties', 'Wops' and 'Mussos.'

So, we grew up with an inexplicable feeling of not belonging, with a furtive urge to deny our origin. We had been given a level of education that our parents had not enjoyed. The age-old problem of children speaking in the language in which they had been schooled had been worsened by the position in which we had found ourselves at the outbreak of war. The speaking of Italian was not high on our priority list.

49. *The young generation:*
Renato & Johnny Pizzamiglio

The long hours of constant toil which our parents had willingly accepted held no attraction for us. We had seen our Scottish friends' family life-style, where work stopped at 5.30pm and at week-ends. For the Scots it seemed that there was a time for work and a time for play: the latter seemingly had no place in an immigrant's way of life. The young Italian generation realised that the only way out of this situation was to avoid being drawn into the 'shop'. The escape was into teaching, nursing, hotel catering, the travel and film industries: the call was varied and far-reaching.

The old generation expected their offspring to marry Italians, wanting them to bring into the family those of the same religion, customs and background. But, in only three cases did members of the Inverness community marry among themselves. Two factors weighed against this inter-marriage. Firstly, unlike the Central Belt and Aberdeen with their Fascio Clubs, in Inverness there was no society, club or other focal point where the Italian community could meet and socialise.

50. Islands Tearoom

Secondly, there was no Catholic Secondary school. So, from an early age, the children of Italian, Catholic parents were brought into contact with the community at large, which was nearly all Protestant. Through participation in secondary school-life, the children were taken out of the closed community resulting in a weakening of the tie to the shop.. Consequently, it is not surprising that about 60% of the second generation married non-Catholics, outside the Italian community. As a result of this intermarriage there was dilution, and, in at least 50% of cases, complete loss of adherence to the Catholic faith and knowledge of the Italian language.

51. New Ness Café

CHAPTER SIXTEEN

Integration

So, with this new intermingling a new term was coined: the Italo-Scot.

Those who did remain in the family business saw its demise as the eating habits of a post-war British public changed. As old Inverness was being demolished the building developers were taking over the town. Bridge Street, where three cafes were located was the first to be demolished. Eastgate with three cafes and a fish restaurant, which had been established since the Twenties, was redeveloped. Businesses were taken over by the new immigrants of the Seventies and Eighties.

Only one remained as it was for over sixty years. The last 'Tally' café in Inverness closed on 2 April 1993—'*Dorando's*, run by Henry (Enrico) Turriani at 89 Academy Street. Changing habits, growing competition and lack of parking space in the centre of the then town had taken its toll on the old family business—opened in the 1920s by the lethargic Renato Turriani, alias Dorando. Some of us still remember its counter-top covered with

52. *Bridge Street*

53. *Eastgate—South*

54. *Eastgate—North*

newspapers, its ice-cream freezer, its jars of sweets lining the shelves, its windows filled with boxes of chocolates or Easter eggs, its open fire in the tea-room giving an intimacy not found in the impersonal eating-places of today. Henry himself says:

> 'It's a relic of the past which really seems to have no place in the fast-food take-away world of today. Yet it lasted my father's life-time, it gave me my livelihood, but that's it—my son wants a different way of life.'

Gradually the second generation of Italian immigrants integrated and with this integration a new sense of identity has come about. And with it, a need to talk about it. The shock of feeling estranged at a very early age from the playmates and country you thought liked you left a mark for life. You found yourself trying to hide your Italianness, hating your very Italian name—although, as my Latin teacher once proclaimed to the class, 'What a wonderful language Italian is that it can turn Nellie Smith into Leonella Ferrari!'

The uncertainty that always troubled me is illustrated by two poets named Robert:

Browning:	*Open my heart and you will see*
	Graved inside of it, 'Italy'.
Burns:	*My heart's in the Highlands wherever I go.*

I understood Italian but refused to speak it. I grew up in no-man's land, a stranger in Italy and a 'Tally' in the land of my birth. They say 'time heals'—and so it has done for the lost generation of Italians who, like me, had to learn that to have an Italian aspect to one's life is a God-sent bonus.

So, quietly, without racial tensions, the third generation of Italo-Scots has become part of Invernessiana and we are now referred to as Scots Italians.

The 'Tallies' have not gone—they are part of us.

55. *Turriani Family—Bianco Renato (Dorando) Henry*

56. *Ferrari Family—Bellfield Park 1949*

APPENDIX

ITALIAN BUSINESSES 1938-39

Extracts from The Burgh Valuation Roll

1 Ness Walk/1A Young Street.....Angelo Canessa.............................Confectioner
Tenant: Pietro Ferrari

8 Church Street............................Loreto Celli.....................................Tailor

36 Church Street ....Renato Turriani............................Confectioner

Queensgate Arcade......................Biagio Candellini
Patrizio Lunardi

24 High Street..............................Victor Conn...................................Restaurateur

17 & 17a Inglis Street..................Victor Conn...................................Confectioner

21 & 23 Inglis Street....................Victor Conn...................................Confectioner

9a Bridge Street ....Peter Bernardi ....Confectioner

29 Bridge Steet............................Peppino Rizza................................Confectioner

35 Castle Street............................Mrs Caterina Bernardi

57 Castle Street............................Luigi Pieraccini

71 Castle Street............................Gino Giubarelli

4 & 6 Eastgate ....Giuseppe Bonici............................Confectioner

30 Eastgate ....Mrs Romola Simonetti (Italy)
Tenant: Biagio Candellini............Confectioner

46a Eastgate ....Enrico Pizzamiglio

31 Academy Street.......................Biagio Candellini
Patrizio Lunardi............................Confectioner

33 Academy Street ....Nicholas W Fornari......................Hairdresser

41 Academy Street ....Primo & Emilio Pieraccini...........Restaurateurs

89 Academy Street ....Renato Turriani

99 Academy Street ....Enrico Pagliari

11 Chapel Street...........................Trustees of Joseph Bergamini
Tenant: Delia Giubarelli ....Confectioner

12 Chapel Street ....J Matti..Dry Cleaner

10 Greig Street ....Secondo Salvadori

7 Wells Street ....Giacomo Persichini

ITALIAN DETAINEES

Inverness Prison 1940

NAME	AGE	HEIGHT (Feet/inches)	BORN
Loreto Celli	48	5.1	Italy
Ottavio Celli	16	5.3	Glasgow
Luigi Cabrelli	41	5.3	Italy
Pietro Ferrari	45	5.3	Italy
Gino Giubarelli	29	5.9	Glasgow
Francesco Guicciari	38	5.2	Italy
Remo Giubarelli	24	5.7	Airdrie
Luigi Pieraccini	32	5.4	Glasgow
Charles Pieraccini	35	5.3	Glasgow
Primo Pieraccini	43	5.4	Italy
Enrico Pizzamiglio	47	5.4	Italy
Antonino Pizzamiglio	35	5.5	Switzerland
Enrico Pagliari	37	5.3	France
Renzo Serafini	25	5.10	Hawick
Victor Serafini	21	5.5	Italy
Enrico Turriani	17	5.7	Italy

ACKNOWLEDGEMENTS

1. Murdoch Rogers	'Italiani in Scozia' in B. Kay(ed.) Odyssey 'Voices from Scotland's Recent Past'
2. Andrew Wilkin	1979 'Origins and Destinations of the Early Italo Scots' Association of Teachers of Italian – 1990 'Introducing the Italo Scots' Vector Universita di Modena
3. Terri Colpi	1991 'The Italian Factor' Mainstream Publishing, (Edinburgh) 1991, 'Italians' Count in Scotland' The St James Press, London 2015
4. R.F.Foerster	'The Italian Emigration of Our Times,' Cambridge, Harvard University Press 1924
5. Wendy Ugolini	2014 Experiencing war as the 'Enemy other' 1998 Interview with Renzo Serafini
6. Peter and Leni Gillman	1980 'Collar the Lot' Quarter Books Ltd. – order attributed to Churchill, page 152, 'regrettable and deplorable things…' page 309 Lord Anderson
7. Italian Detainees	With kind permission of the Keeper of the Records of Scotland – Extract from Index of Male Prisoners for Inverness Prison
8. Mark Twain	The Innocents Abroad 1869, ch.19
9. Dante Alighieri	The Divine Comedy – *Paradiso* xvii, *Inferno* v
10. Rachel Pistol	'Enemy Alien and Refugee: conflicting Identities in Great Britain during the Second World War'. University of Sussex Journal of Contemporary History 16, pp.37–58
11. Tudor Allen	Little Italy – The Story of London's Italian Quarter

12. Parliamentary Committee on Sunday Trading 1906

13. Slater's Directory of Inverness 1911

14. Oxford Journals, European Review of Economic History. Vol.4

NEWSPAPERS

The Daily Mirror	26 April 1940
The Highland News	18 May 1940, 15 June 1940, 22 June 1940
The Northern Chronicle	29 May 1940, 12 June 1940
The Evening News	11 June 1940

IMAGE ACKNOWLEDGEMENTS

With kind permission of:

Disegno di Benito Jacovitti, Roma .... 'The Emigrant'

Highland Photographic Archive, ... Rendezvous Cafe, Dorando's
Inverness Museum and Art Gallery

Highland Archives and Am Baile .... Bridge Street

Camden Local Studies and Archives Centre .... Ice cream seller
Holburn Library London WC1 8PA   Organ grinder

Mrs Dorothy Morrison, Inverness .... Washington Soda Fountain
                                                     Eastgate – views

Inverness Remembered .... Old Ness Café
                                                     Eastgate

Sergio Serafini, Inverness .... The Locarno Café

Mrs Isobel Pieraccini, Inverness .... The Highland Restaurant

Mrs Maria Pagliari .... Enrico Pagliari
                                                     & Ferrari children